A Portrait of Virginia A. Smith

**GAINING STRENGTH
THROUGH LIFE'S JOURNEY**

A Portrait of Virginia A. Smith

GAINING STRENGTH THROUGH LIFE'S JOURNEY

By Virginia A. Smith
Copyright © 2017

Copyright © 2017
by Virginia A. Smith

All rights reserved. No part of this book may be reprinted or reproduced in any form or by any electronic, mechanical, or other means, now known or hereafter invented, including photocopy, recording, and information storage and retrieval, without permission in writing from the author.

ISBN: 978-0-9996746-9-7
Library of Congress Control Number: 2017961526

Designed and Published by:
The Solid Foundation Group, LLC
PO Box 1483
Smyrna, GA 30081
www.TheSolidFoundationGroup.com

Printed in the United States of America

Dedications

To my son, the late Herbert "Ricky" LaCoste Clemons, who is the stimulus behind this book. Having received years of encouragement (in person and through his written letters), Ricky was the inspiration for me deciding to share my life story in hopes of encouraging others. I am truly blessed to have given birth, raised and known such a thoughtful and inquisitive son and young man, who truly showered me with his purest love and support.

Acknowledgements

I'd like to first acknowledge and thank God for giving me the insight, the testimonies, the strength and courage to write.

Secondly, I'd like to pay tribute to all the persons who have encouraged me and prayed that I didn't lose heart: my late son, Herbert (Ricky), who persistently told me to write, even in letters he had written to me years before he departed this life; my youngest daughter, Shundra, my dream maker and pusher who is there for every accomplishment in my life; Shundra's husband, Marvin, who supports me in every way; my grandson, Joshua, for his inspiration, his youthful ideas, his belief in me and help with my writing; and my grandson, Micah, for constantly giving me hugs, kisses, and affirmations that I am doing a good job.

In addition, I'd like to offer a special thanks to my spiritual support: Wajeehah C. Jefferson, a strong supporter; Rev. Dr. Bennie Rivers who spent many late nights helping me give birth to this Portrait; Dee Dee Moulder for her friendship and support; and Rev. Dr. Sherryl Powell for always being there for me, for praying that God stirs the gifts within me, for keeping me encouraged and for assisting me with the progression of this manuscript.

I'd also like to acknowledge my only sister, Jackie, as she has always said, "I knew one day you would be a singer or a writer."; my brother, Walter, for being an excellent motivator from childhood through my college journey; and The Solid Foundation Group for turning my dreams into a pleasant reality.

To my mother, the late Fannie Lou Smith-Vaughn, and my father, the late Walter Allen Smith (who loved me without limits), thank you for giving me life. To Mrs. Hazel Irvin (who at the time of this book is 90 years old) for being my friend, mentor and mother for over 25 years; and last, but not least, the true love of my life, the late Lonnie Warren. You were my fiancé, but we will always be married in my heart.

Foreword

Insightful, thought provoking, yet told in a comfortable, casual, and sometimes comedic fashion, this book is a "must read" for women. Told as one woman's story, A Portrait of Virginia A. Smith is the story that contains the fabric from which many women's lives have been woven. It tells of the hereditary dysfunction or disturbance in the usual pattern of activity or behavior of families or familial relationships that at the time seems normal, but is excruciatingly painful; yet, at the same time is filled with moments of great joy and laughter.

This disturbance is systemic and significantly impacts views, self-perceptions as well as esteem, and fosters cyclical behavior in the struggle to fill the void of the unknown missing ingredient of life. On the other hand, in running away from the current situation, due to limited information, many a woman has found herself in unexpected predicaments. It is these very predicaments that summon character, forge wisdom and from which women gain their strength.

Although, I'm not sure if dysfunction is the right word because it seems as if irregularity in the functioning of family, disturbance of normal or expected patterns is itself "the norm" in most families (and especially in the African American family); yet, somehow, we survive.

Reading this book is like sitting down to a cup of coffee, tea, cake, and laughter with Virginia herself, as she shares her story; however, facing it, embracing it, and celebrating the wonderful person that she has become (as a result of all of it) is what is gleaned most from reading this delightful story of Mrs. Virginia A. Smith's portrait! Enjoy!

Rev. Dr. Sherryl L. Powell

Just as many of the most precious jewels often lie just beneath the surface and even some very deep below the surface, you can't determine the quality of the stone until you examine and explore the value of the stone. And, so it is with human life. We can never determine the character or spiritual make-up of individuals by the way they look, what they wear, the way they talk, who they know, where they live or where they go to church. The only way to know who lives above the surface is to get to know them through their challenges and their joyful moments.

I was one of Virginia's professors at Beulah Heights Bible College (now Beulah Heights University). I read her papers and evaluated her communication skills within the classroom setting and her engaging attributes with her fellow classmates and myself. I've also worshipped with her at Cosmopolitan A.M.E. Church. However, I realized after reading her book that I had no idea who the "real" Virginia Smith was during the 1990's. I did not have a clue of the severe challenges she faced in life from birth to the beginning of the 21st Century.

Virginia's spiritual birthing pains were difficult, hard, problematic, grim, prolonged. It's hard to believe her powerful presence today without recognizing her presence being wrapped up and tied up in the Lord. The grace of God has not allowed the weapons of warfare to prevail against her because she's the KING's Kid and she is a WINNER, as revealed in this book.

I thank God for using her departed son, Herbert Clemons, to encourage her to write and share with us "A Portrait of Virginia A. Smith." Read, Learn and Enjoy the life story of Reverend Virginia A. Smith.

Wajeehah Cynthia Jefferson

Prologue

I'm presently considered an elder in life – fully blossomed and ready to share some of the milestones conquered in my 75 years here on earth. With the encouragement of my son, Ricky, who would constantly say, "Mama, you need to write about your story. It will be just like giving birth to a child."

As I reflect on his sincere urge for me to write about my journey through life, I finally sat down one day (three years after his appalling death from diabetes complications) and began this portrait of my three score and fifteen years.

****

Hi. I'm Virginia, born into this world on December 1, 1941 at 4:24 am at Grady Hospital in Atlanta, Georgia, to the late Walter Allen and Fannie Lou Smith. I was the fourth of six children: one older sister, Jackie; two older brothers, Walter and Lamar; and two younger brothers, Lester and Donald.

My life's journey has been a combination of fear, shyness, timidity, and disappointments. My first mentor, encourager and teacher was my late father. He saw something in me that I did not see within myself. I owe so much to him and to my Heavenly Father, who transformed my life, healed my heart and encouraged me with this song that continues to guide my everyday life:

> "There's something more to me than I can see.
> There's something more to you than you can see.
> But there's a need to be challenged
> That you may blossom you see.
> There is something more to us than we can see."

This book is written with every reader in mind that they may be encouraged, inspired, and enlightened by the strokes from the brush that so delicately paint my portrait.

Inside will be reflections of my life: the joys as well as the dark places and traumatic times that helped mold me into being the woman I am today. Reflections often take me to places I don't want to go because revisiting those places has caused all of the hurt, shame, anger, guilt, and other traumatic experiences to resurface, which is like revisiting the pain all over again.

You may be asking, 'why visit those places?' Well, you see, the joy behind all of this is that my whole life wasn't a life full of pain. I've seen on many occasions how – during it all – God has been right there making sure I "made it through." This is how I can now write to you…helping you understand why I think, act, and live the way I do.

Table of Contents

The Sketches

    My Dad.. 3
    My Mother... 9
    My Childhood...19

Colors, Highlights, Shadows & Smudges

    Growing Up...29
    My Marriages...41
    Walking in Faith..65
    My Inspiration...81
    My Calling..99

The Perfect Frame

    In Retrospect..105

The Sketches

*Before I formed you in the womb
I knew you, before you were born I set you apart...
Jeremiah 1:5 NIV*

VIRGINIA A. SMITH

My Dad

My dad, Mr. Walter Allen Smith, was a very gentle and mild-mannered man who worked as a freight hauler for Georgia Highway Freight Company in Atlanta, Georgia.

It seemed as though my dad and my mother's roles were reversed; he was more nurturing and patient, and never really raised his voice, except for when he would get tired of my mother's yelling. He would then stand in the middle of the room and shout loudly, "Ahhhhhhh Fongoola!" That was the only time I would ever hear him yell.

Dad was an artist and a singer. He would often sing Jazz around the house, and read every kind of book from Shakespeare to Sports to Philosophy to Religion. He would play lots of fun, quirky games and activities with us, like entering the room imitating "The Hunchback of Notre Dame." He had the walk and growl down perfectly, which made us all scream; but, he would get the biggest laugh.

My dad also had us performing mock spelling bees and poem recitals, and would even let us play and record songs on the reel-to-reel tape recorder.

Dad was always saying funny things to us and was good at making everyone laugh. He was also a very intellectual man, even though he only had an eighth-grade education. He would often draw, teach us to sing, and read poetry to us; but, what really stood out to me was the poem, "The Raven," by Edger Allen Poe. My dad would get quite dramatic when reading that poem, so much so that it would capture our undivided attention – every time.

When we would get into trouble my dad would never yell, but used psychology to talk to us. He told us he could touch the top of our heads and tell who was lying. And, although he never went to church with us (because he was raised in the Church of God in Christ and we went to a Baptist Church), he was always encouraging us, saying that we could be anything we wanted to be. My father never had a negative word to say about and/or to anyone. He was always positive, and was likened to the Pied Piper in the community. All of the kids loved him (even when he was drunk). The kids would run down the street saying, "We got you, Mr. Da".

My father was given several nicknames such as: Mr. Da, Big Jim, the Professor, and Old Blessed. My father's closest friends would call him, 'Big Jim'; and to this day, I still wonder why they called him that. He was not a big man.

The names, 'Old Blessed' and 'The Professor,' came from the medical interns at Morehouse College who were serving their internships at Grady Hospital during the time my father was hospitalized there. Those interns enjoyed talking with my father on a daily basis, as they gleaned wisdom and insights about life and their studies.

My dad was in the hospital for about a month. I remember him telling us when he entered that he would not be back. We (my brothers and I) said, "Oh, Da, don't say that."

He would simply respond, "No, I will not be back. My time is up. I am out of here; I am doomed."

Having had many surgeries, the doctors often said they had never had a patient that was so strong. My father withstood two surgeries within two days; and unfortunately, even after these two surgeries, they still could not stop the internal bleeding he was experiencing.

One day, I went to the hospital after work and was sitting in the chair looking at the blood running into him. My father asked me, "Are you scared?"

I replied, "No."

He then said, "Read what is written on the bag that contains the blood."

I replied, "the bag says, Whole Human Blood," and then waited for him to comment.

He then said, "The good thing is that it is not animal blood." He was so dramatic when he said it, we both just laughed and laughed. It did relax and calm me down, though. He knew I was nervous.

His last request was to see all of his children together at one time. My sister, Jackie, had just left and made it back to her home in New Jersey; and my brother, Walter, was in Spain, with only one way to find him – through the Red Cross. They both managed to get back to Atlanta right away, though.

My father joked with us; but, he was serious when letting us know he would not be coming back home. Of course, we did not believe him at that time, even though we could see how he was struggling to talk (because he had a breathing tube inserted down his throat). Despite his attempts to stay positive, we could see the tears in his eyes.

What we did not know at the time is that he was actually dying, even as he was trying to speak. He would not yield to death's call, however, until we all left the hospital the next day.

My father died of a peptic ulcer on January 26, 1969.

I remember dreaming about him many times afterwards, and waking up crying. I did this almost every night until one night I was dreaming the reoccurring dream that he was in a casket at his funeral. In this particular night's dream, however, he rose up and with that famous smile, looked at me and said, "Baby girl, don't cry anymore. I am alright." And then, he laid back down.

I never dreamed of him again after that.

…

My Mother

My mother, Mrs. Fannie Lou Smith, was a stern and serious woman who rarely laughed. She was a hard worker who tended to work too much and too hard sometimes. But, the thing I remember most is that she yelled and fussed a lot – for just about everything; and, that she was often very mean and believed in belts and switches – far more than my dad.

As I grew up, my mother would tell me how I wanted so much of her attention that she would just lay me on the bed while she finished cooking or working around the house. She said I'd kick and scream the whole time (all day sometimes); but, when my father got home, he would pick me up and I'd look at her over his shoulder and frown at her. When she told me that, I said, "Mother, you know babies don't know how to frown like that."

She replied, "Well, you did. And, you would do that every time your father picked you up."

That was a consistent story shared about the first few months of my life. As a toddler my Aunt Ruth said I still followed behind my mother, crying to be picked up. Aunt Ruth (who was always around until she moved to New Jersey) would ask my mother often, "Why don't you pick that baby up, so she can stop crying?" Mother would simply respond, "I don't have time."

From other stories told I don't believe my mother ever picked me up. Being the fourth of six children left very little time for her to tend to me.

As long as I can remember, I always thought that my mother never really liked me, because she was never affectionate towards me. This – honestly - made me not really like her either.

It still puzzles me as to why she disliked me so. I tried to do everything that she would tell me to do. At one point when I was younger, I used to think that maybe it was because I was born with a lot of hair all over me.

According to my mother, my Aunt Ruth once said to her, "Lou, you know, you've kind-of run out now from having babies. This baby has so much hair on her she looks like a monkey. You should stop having babies."

My mother – though insulted – said she didn't quite know how to respond to my Aunt Ruth (and honestly, I don't even know if she ever responded and or what her response was).

Speaking of my hairiness, my mom has also told me stories of how my dad and a friend he worked with at the Freight Company would often bring home quarts of olive oil. Now, according to my mother, she didn't know if my father and his friend stole this olive oil or bought the olive oil. All I know is that when they'd bring the olive oil home, Mother made a point to bathe me in this oil, as a means of seeing if she could get the hair to shed off. She would do this every other day, making sure there was plenty of oil for me to soak in. I believed she did this because she didn't want too many people seeing her hairy child, which led me to believe that she was embarrassed of me.

After months of being bathed in the olive oil, hair actually began shedding off of me. My hair began to come off in all of the places she didn't think hair should be, leaving me with hair in all the right places, such as my eyebrows, eyelashes, and head. She said my Aunt Ruth came back to say to her, "Well, now the baby is beginning to look normal." Aunt Ruth always spoke her mind; that was just who she was.

Other instances of when I felt my mom disliked me was when my Dad would sit up on many nights in front of the heater just to keep me warm, or when I would speak at certain times. I think she (just like my sister, Jackie) thought I sounded so much like him that it bothered her. My sister, Jackie, would always say to me, "You sound just like Da...Go head on, Old Blessed."

No matter how many stories I can think of, I still can't honestly narrow down exactly why mother disliked me so much. Out of six children, my mother had one favorite and it was not me. It was my brother, Lester. I say this because he agreed with everything she said or did

Mother never showed any pride in any of my accomplishments as a child or as an adult, although I would always invite her to events that I participated in.

Our relationship became strained even more after I became an adult. She was always criticizing me and saying negative things to me, such as, "You are too fat! You don't look well. You must not be resting at night." And, she always had an angle or motive for wanting to do things for me that I didn't ask for.

She also wasn't very encouraging in helping with my achievements. Her words to me (said frequently) was, "You can't do that..."

But, no matter how I'd like to continue painting this negative picture of my mother, she actually did do many good deeds for me when I was younger.

She was good with her hands. We always ate well because my mother was a wonderful cook (a real Martha Stewart of her day). She would even put fresh-cut flowers on the table (I still remember those Gladiolas).

When she was a waitress and served big parties at large hotels, we would always look forward to her bringing us cakes and pieces of the restaurant's best cut steaks. She also catered the pastor's events and other church related functions.

When I was in school dances and needed a costume, she would go the extra mile to make all my costumes for various school activities. So, you see, she did do some good things for me.

After five of us had already left the house, my mother remarried and became Mrs. Vaughan. My youngest brother (who at the time was about 12 or 13) was the only one left at home with them.

When I left, I felt free of all the hurt and disappointment I would so often experience. In my late thirties, I remember sitting in Sunday School while my teacher, Evangelist Georgie Burgess, was teaching on forgiveness. She stayed on that lesson for weeks, even though it was only supposed to last one week. She told the class that it was s topic she could not let go of.

These classes prompted me to one day ask the question, "How do you forgive someone if they continue doing the same thing?" After not getting a response, I further asked, "What if it is a family member?" (I was beating around the bush because I didn't want my teacher or anyone else to know that my questions were really about my mother).

From those Sunday School lessons, my spirit felt free to go to my Mother and not only forgive her, but ask her to forgive me for all the negative things I may have thought and did. I told her that God had revealed to me that she was the woman he chose to bring me into this world, and that she was not to be the mother I *wanted* her to be; but, instead, the mother that He chose for me.

I was so fired up that I could not stop talking. I guess I talked to much, though, because I can remember her abruptly guiding me to the door saying, "It is getting late, so you better head home."

As I was driving away, I was so happy that I sang all the way home. I felt so free. I would visit and talk to her after that; but, I was determined to keep my distance.

When my brother, Lester (her favorite) had a stroke, my mother didn't know if he would live or die soon. Because of this, she went to the bank and put my name on her account. Despite how she acted, she always knew she could trust me. She even carried me to the funeral home as she made her own funeral arrangements.

The last years of her life I noticed that she had stopped going to church and rarely wanted to leave home. Her mind was getting weak, which led me to being with her almost every day – writing checks for bills, cashing her checks (she always checked the account number before she signed it), going grocery shopping, and cooking every day. I even had someone drive me to get her groceries, when I fell and broke my wrist – all up until the time it was healed.

I remember sitting with her one day as she talked about when I was a baby, not so much about me as a little girl. She would also tell me things that she had done for others in the family, and then say to me, "I did nothing for you. I went to Lester's graduations and all of his achievements, but I never went to nothing that you were in." And, then look at me as if she wanted a response. I didn't know what to say, so I said nothing. I never trusted her or her motives.

That would prompt her to ask, "Did you hear what I said?"

I would simply reply, "yes, Mother, that was your money and you did what you wanted to do with it."

She would often talk about the things she did. Many of the times I would be with her, she did most of the talking. I would just listen, although she did like when I sang hymns and reminisce of the songs we'd sing when we were in the choir together.

She would often start conversations with, "Who would have thought that you would have been the one to…" and, then, change the subject.

I remember having no emotions during that time. I think it was because we didn't have a mother-daughter bond. I was just doing what came naturally to me, and she would sometimes make a mistake and say a sharp word that was kind of mean because it came naturally to her (remember she still didn't like me). But, then, she would say, "Oh, I am so sorry. I didn't mean that."

I would just reassure my mother by responding, "no words can hurt or keep me away. As long as God gives me breath I will be here every day because you are my mother." And I meant that from my heart.

On February 12, 2014, the coldest day of the year, I found out my mother had passed. I remember calling her to see how she was doing the night before and the day of; but, she never answered. I was starting to get worried, because I felt something must be wrong. I immediately called a church member, Sharon, who lived around the corner from my mother. I asked if she could just talk to me, because my mother is not answering the phone.

Her husband, Julius, volunteered to walk around the corner to my mom's house, and came back saying there was no answer at the door.

They both then walked to the fire station and called me to confirm to the police that I was a family member. This gave them permission to enter my mom's home. They found my mom lying in her bed (where she transitioned), with her robe lying folded near her.

The police officer came to pick me up, since their vehicles were equipped for the weather. It felt really strange to me to be sitting there waiting for the coroner to come to her house. Luckily, Sharon and her husband stayed with me the whole time, even up to the moments they were preparing to remove my mom's body. I had to leave the room for that part, however, because I didn't want to see it.

I remember having feelings of emptiness; but, kept my mind busy by thinking about all of the things that needed to be done in preparation for her funeral. I was glad my brother came over from Alabama to help; but, he went back immediately after everything was over.

My Childhood

"...for I know the plans I have for you." declares the LORD, "plans to prosper you and not to harm you, plans to give you hope and a future."
Jeremiah 29:11 NIV

I was born at 383 Gray Street in Atlanta, Georgia. Shortly after my birth, we moved right down the street to Herndon Home Projects (466 John Street, Apt. 319). The projects weren't a bad place to live; the bedrooms were upstairs and the living room and kitchen downstairs.

It's hard to believe that I still remember the exact address and telephone number after all these years. I think they stick with me because it was my first home and the neighborhood was quite memorable. The floors were concrete, and very cold in the winter. Every apartment had its own fenced-in backyard and was heated by a radiator located downstairs. Sometimes we would put clothes on the radiator to dry; and sometimes, before going upstairs to bed, we would sit in front of it to keep warm. That's how cold it was.

When mother and dad weren't home, we found all kinds of things to get into. My sister, Jackie, and brother, Lamar, would get a pillow and sheet and slide down the stairs. One night, my brother was sliding down the stairs and slid right into my mother at the bottom. We all fell out laughing; but, Mother did not find that funny at all. We were all punished with the belt.

Another time, I remember me and my brother, Lester, being outside in the backyard, while the others were entertaining themselves inside. We were making a tent over the clothes' lines in the backyard. The blanket we used to make the tent was a wool Army blanket. We threw it over the clothes line in the backyard to hide from our brothers and sister. We thought if they found us, we would then pretend that we were asleep; but, we stayed there pretending for so long that we actually ended up falling asleep.

The others went to bed and left us outside (probably forgetting that we were still out there). My mother came home from work and did her usual count of all of the children (which she did every night although, at that time, it was only five of us). Realizing two of us were missing, she searched for us, eventually finding us in the backyard under the tent. She was so angry, but probably more scared. And, as usual, we were met with the belt that night. too.

So, as you can see, we totally amused ourselves in ways that sometimes resulted in us getting into trouble, as well.

Years pass fast; but, of course, when you are young it doesn't appear that way. I remember being at the age of five and getting ready to attend kindergarten at Davis Street Elementary (now named, Mary M. Bethune Elementary School).

Walter, my oldest brother, was in charge of picking me up every day. One day he was late, and I was the only child left at school. I remember sitting on the steps crying and thinking that no one would ever come for me, and that I would be left alone forever without my family (I always thought the worst).

Shortly after having those thoughts, I looked up and saw my brother walking rather briskly towards me. Since he was late picking me up, that meant he would be late going to work, if we didn't move fast. He always worked after school. At that time, it would always seem like he was so much older than me; but, in reality, he was only six years older than me.

As a young girl, I also remember having a strong craving for sweets. If I saw dessert prepared, I would lose my appetite, as I would much rather eat the dessert than my dinner. Being a very picky eater who ate very little, my family nicknamed me, "Bird." I was actually skinny as a young kid, and would get sick if my mother made me eat.

Another issue I remembered was me - around the age of six or seven – having very sensitive eyes (so much so that sunlight really bothered me). I would frown often because my eyes would hurt so bad.

One Easter, I can recall my father taking pictures of the family outside; he always took pictures with his box camera. My mother kept yelling at me to stop frowning, which in turn made me cry. And, to my rescue, my father walked over, stooped down to me and said, "Baby girl, if you don't stop crying, do you know what will happen when you grow up?"

I said, whimpering, "No."

He said, "When you grow up you won't have water left in your body to pee." His comment forced me to smile, even though my eyes were still burning. I didn't know how to explain to my parents what horrible effects the sun had on my eyes; but, those vision challenges led me to wearing glasses – even to this day.

Around the age of eight or nine, I remember going into the grocery store where my father worked on the weekends. I had one dime that would purchase one cake; but, because I wanted two cakes, I had one cake in my hand and had hid the other cake in my pocket.

Unbeknownst to me, the store owner asked me about the one in my pocket. I was so scared I almost peed on myself. How could he have known?

I told him I was going to pay for it, not knowing anyone could see through that lie. He told me to take it and go home. I thought I had gotten away with trying to steal the cake; but, the owner told my father about what happened, and that was the first and last spanking I ever received from my father (which really was just one pop, as my father did not spank me or my sister...just my brothers). And before you ask the question, the answer is, no, I never stole anything ever again.

As a little girl, growing up in a family of church-going people, I would attend church sometimes with my friends and they would often go with me to my church, as well. I remember one time I was with my two friends and we were on program to sing together at Mt. Vernon Baptist Church on Northside Drive. The song we sang was, "Where Jesus Leads Me I Will Follow," which I was singing as if I was the only one around...really giving it my all. This was actually out of character for me, which made it a strange experience.

I learned to attend church regularly by example. I was always up early and dressed for Sunday School, before everyone else in the house. We'd have to walk about a mile to First Corinth Baptist church; but, I was always eager to attend Sunday School because I admired and adored my teacher.

I thought she was so pretty and very nice, and she made me feel as if I was the only one in her class. Her name is Mrs. Jessie Vinson. She is in her nineties now and still teaching. She treated all of us in her class the same; but, I think I felt it more personally because I needed her attention.

My mother was a member of a choir named, the Corinthian Chorus. When I was young, I remember saying how when I grow up, I, too, was going to join the Corinthian Chorus, because they sang so well. I liked to see them march in on Sunday mornings. They could really sing and the musician, Ms. Mattie Murphy, was a gifted pianist.

When I grew up, I did get into that choir and I enjoyed singing with them. It was a mixed group and some of my friends were with me.

I really liked traveling and sitting with the older women as we sang on the bus. I remember often asking a certain woman if she could sing a certain song. She would respond, "Aren't you tired of hearing that same old song?" But, since I really liked to hear her sing, "Remember Me," she always said ok and sang it to me again.

My mother was a member of a local Social and Savings club in our neighborhood. They'd meet annually, and I'd have to attend because my sister did not want to go. Mother would put me on the program to recite a poem and my dad always taught me the poems before each event.

The ladies would say how good I was, and my mother would smile and say, "Thank you. That's my Virginia;" but when we'd leave, she never smiled at me.

I used to love to attend Sunday School church teas, club teas and choir teas with my mother, because it seems that was the only time she would be nice to me. I wanted her to like me.

When mother would prepare fancy sandwiches for catering jobs, I'd assist her by cutting the ends of the bread slices, preparing the various spreads, wrapping and putting them in the freezer before slicing and arranging them in boxes. The benefit of doing this work led me to learning her recipes and her style, which I continued using even with my children. I've made many sandwiches since that time in my life, and even mastered my mom's famous banana pudding with egg white meringue.

Although I didn't like being yelled at during the process of learning, I actually enjoyed developing the delicate skill of preparing food. And, after over sixty years of doing so, I can now prepare many dishes on demand.

Colors, Highlights, Shadows and Smudges

"You don't have enough faith," Jesus told them. "I tell you the truth, if you had faith even as small as a mustard seed, you could say to this mountain, 'Move from here to there,' and it would move. Nothing would be impossible."
Matthew 17:20 NIV

Growing Up

As a teen, I began to be a little more open. I started talking a little more; but I was still shy. I've always believed my mother had a problem with me because of how my father interacted with me from the time I was a baby. She told me that Da would sit up sometimes all night and hold me in front of the heater under the covers so that I would stay warm, despite her telling him to put me to bed. He would always respond, "if I lay her down she'll kick the cover off and catch cold."

Mother said I was a sickly baby who would get very ill when I had a cold. I believe she resented that and somehow resented me. I think I probably was my dad's favorite – only because I was the only one of the children who listened to him and believed everything he tried to teach us.

I remember one time he was teaching us about believing in ourselves. He was telling all of us if we just believe, we can do anything. My brother, Lamar, asked, "Anything?"

Da said, "You see that building we lived in while in the projects?"

We all said, "yes."

"If you believe, do you know you can move that building...but, only if you believe it so?"

When it was time for us to go to bed, Lamar, who was always joking asked me, "I bet you believe everything Da said?"

I responded, "yes, cause it's true."

Lamar said, "Ok, show me how you gonna do it."

I got so upset that I started crying, because I could not explain how. I just believed I could do it. He laughed at me.

Whatever my dad was teaching us I was interested in hearing. Even if I couldn't understand it, I wanted to learn – poetry, singing, spelling contests and him teaching me to dance.

I was the only one who wanted to dance as a ballerina, ballroom and waltz dancer. Da taught me these dances by putting my feet on top of his and moving to the music. He even taught me how to bow after the dances.

The first time my father left home I was about nine or ten. He was going to New Jersey to live with his sister.

He sat all of us down and told us he had to leave for a while, and that he wanted us to be good. All of us were sobbing and really begging him to not leave us. He was crying with us, all at the same time hugging and continuing to tell us he had to leave.

My mother was upstairs and never came downstairs. I was deeply saddened because my life line was now gone. After almost a year he wanted to come back home; so, he and Mother asked my grandmother for monies so that he could get back home.

We never knew the circumstances of him leaving; but, we were extremely happy he was home again. You see, my father was love, joy, and happiness, as well as discipline to us. He gave each of us what we needed.

He left again when I was in about the ninth grade. I think that time Mother put him out. I don't know if he was working or not; but he would come every day to see us.

Mother told us not to let him in because he didn't want us anyway.

Well, when Mother left for work most days, we would let Da know she was gone and let him in to eat, sleep, and spend time with us before she got home.

She – one day – found out and told us we better not ever let him in again. We were afraid after that; but, I remember Lester and I taking turns after school to watch for when Mother would come home, so that Da could leave in time.

I don't remember whether my mother ever just sat and talked with me about anything while growing up. She worked full time and part time; so, conversation was always… "Is my uniform ready? Go pay this bill and take care of your brothers and Tina." …so, we did not have a relationship. We didn't have a mother-daughter bond. I always figured I was there to do what I was told; so, I settled with that, and never expected any more.

I do remember running away from home when I was around the age of 13 or 14, however. I was so tired of my mother fussing at me and calling me names that one evening I hid in the closet and waited until she went to her night job. I called my father, and told him I needed to leave and come live with him. He told me to catch the bus and come to the store where he worked.

Once I got there, he gave me his key. He only had one bedroom, but, said for me to wait there until he got off from work. He worked just around the corner from where he lived.

When he got home he brought me a sandwich and him a quart of beer, and immediately began asking me questions such as, "what was wrong?" and "was I in a family way (a phrase used in those times to ask if someone was pregnant)?"

I told him, no, and that I never wanted to go back; but, he said he only had one room, the neighborhood was bad, and I was a girl, so he couldn't keep me. He also went on to talk about how I'd be alright with my mother, as she means well. That's what he always said; but, I never understood those words, nor did I accept it as being ok. I felt she was mean and heartless.

That night, he slept in a chair and I slept in his bed. The next day he carried me home.

I don't know what they talked about; but, after he left I heard my mother on the phone talking to one of her friends. She said, "That girl called herself running away from home to her dad's and he didn't want her; so, he brought her right back. There is no telling what he could have done to her." How could she think such a thing?

Tears began to form in my eyes and I dashed into the closet to escape my mother's hurtful words. I hid there and sobbed quietly till there was nothing left.

We ended up moving shortly after that and I was so happy, because I was able to attend David T. Howard High School, instead of Booker T. Washington. I really didn't want to go to Washington High. I missed many days of school, though, because Mother made me stay home to care for both my niece, Tina, and my baby brother, who was two years younger than Tina. My sister left home when Tina was maybe three years old and did not send for her until Tina was about eight or nine years old. Tina was always such a sweet little girl, though; so, I didn't mind.

I remember begging my sister to take me with her. She said she would come back and get me when she got a job, and asked that I take care of her baby and not tell Mother where she was. I would sit on the porch every day and wait for her to come back; but, she never did.

I was responsible for taking Tina and my baby brother to get their shots, for registering them for school, for helping them with their homework, and for sometimes attending PTA meetings for my brother, Lester, who was about eleven years old.

In the neighborhood, we had a recreation center where teens could go dancing. I think we paid about ten cents to go to the dances. My brother, Lamar, and I loved to dance. We were really good dancers, and won many of the dance contests. My sister Jackie didn't dance; she was more of a 'tomboy,' as they called it at that time.

My siblings and I really didn't fight each other like most families did, although my sister would try to fight my oldest brother sometimes, when he wasn't at the Lucky Strike Bowling Alley or The Varsity. He worked a lot because he liked money and buying nice things.

Every summer in the neighborhood, we had what we called, 'May Day.' I think it was around the first week of May. We used to believe if you washed your hair on the day of the first May rain, it would grow. I don't know if that actually worked, however.

We had Kool-Aid, lemonade, cookies, and played a game called, Platting the May-Pole. In this game, we were positioned boy, girl, boy, girl, holding different colors of ribbon. When the music played, we'd go around the pole and plat the ribbon, going over and under as we danced around the pole. This was a European holiday often celebrated in the States and was lots of fun.

Some Saturdays we (my sister and brothers) received a movie treat. We would get our 10 cents and head to the "Fabulous Fox Theater." We had to walk what seemed like two or three miles to the movies, and Blacks couldn't go in the front door at that time; so, we had to go through the side door and walk up those high steps (which were about six flights). When we reached the top, there were only a few rows at the top balcony which were where we – the Blacks – had access to sit. With all of this being said, we wanted to get there early enough to get a seat, and didn't even care about the steps. The only thing we thought about (because we didn't know any differently), was that we were going to watch a movie and enjoy the fun of going.

As a teen, I'd sit on the porch and day dream a lot. I dreamt about my future family which had two children that had a sandbox and a tennis court in the backyard; but, my biggest dream was to visit Paris, France, because I thought that's where love was. My vision of Paris was that it was a carefree and happy environment where everyone walked and held hands. I really wanted and needed to feel loved.

When school had ended for the summer, I asked my mother if I could attend the summer school program at English Avenue Elementary School. The school is now owned by Greater Vine City Opportunities Program, Inc. (founded by "Able" Mable Thomas, who has served as State Representative and City Counsel woman for many years in Georgia).

I'd take crochet, knitting, clay pottery, ballet, and tap-dancing classes. I was so happy to have somewhere to go, as it would allow me to leave home and get out among other youth. This gave me time to work my way out of being so timid, fearful and overly sensitive, and was actually the beginning of my creative journey.

My mother, as mentioned previously, was what I called, mean. She called me names. She always called me black, saying things like, "You little black heifer." You see, during that time it was considered using a curse word when someone called you black. She always yelled at me and I'd go into a corner and cry. I had extremely thick hair and when she combed my hair I would slide down in the chair because it would hurt so bad. She would just pop me with that black comb and say, "you need to stop crying as if your feelings are hurt, because you'll learn people don't care about your feelings."

I thought to myself, "But you're my mother. You ought not want to hurt me." Parents need to be aware of how words can hurt and cut so deeply. The word, "black", stuck with me, and I grew up believing I was extremely dark. So much so that when I looked in the mirror, I actually saw dark skin.

Now, thus far, it may sound like my mother is the evil one and my dad was Mr. Perfect. No, he was a long way from being perfect; but, he had a positive influence on my life. He always encouraged me by telling me I could do anything, and I could be whatever I wanted to be (if I believed). He would also constantly assure me that I was a pretty little girl.

I found out two weeks before I was supposed to graduate from high school that I was one unit short on a math course, which meant that I could not graduate with my class. I thought marching to receive a blank piece of paper was nothing anyway, so I didn't go the last week of school (teen-aged thinking, I know).

I did go back some years later to receive my high school diploma, however, and my dad was the only one at my graduation. Right after my graduation, I remember going to Pascal's Restaurant to get a sandwich. He said to me, "I know you don't like big gifts, so I brought you this small one."

It was a bottle of Chanel N°5 perfume, which I, of course, at that time, had no idea of the value and class of this small little bottle of perfume; but, amazingly, I still use Chanel N°5 to this day.

My Marriages

*There is a time for everything,
and a season for every activity under the heavens:
Ecclesiastes 3:1 NIV*

I and two of my friends were at a teen jam session one Sunday evening at a night club called, Royal Peacock on Auburn Avenue. On Sunday evenings, teens could go there from five to six thirty. I lied to my mother, and told her we were going to the movies. You see, I was not so innocent.

My friends and I saw three guys while at the Royal Peacock, each picking out the guy we liked. And, seeing how my friends were not shy at all, one of them walked over and spoke to one of the guys, saying "my friend wants to meet the tall guy." That friend she was talking about was me.

I only saw this guy from the back. He was tall, dark and kind of handsome and I said, "That is going to be my husband." Be careful what you speak out of your mouth when you have no idea what you are saying.

The other guy went to get him. He came to the table and asked, "Which one of you broads (I had never heard that term before) want to meet me?"

They pointed to me and said, "She's the one."

He said, "My name is Herb. What's yours?"

I said, "Ann." Then, we exchanged phone numbers.

Since it was getting late, my friends and I had to leave. All three guys walked us to the bus stop. Herb told me while walking that he would have taken us home; but his car was in the shop. That was later found to be the first of many lies that he told me.

I must have been about 17, because I was still in school. He had been in the Army, so he had to be about four or five years older. We started, as we called it, 'going together.' When my mother first saw him, she didn't like him; but, she didn't like my two friends either.

We (me, my friends, and the three guys) would all go for rides in one of the guy's car. It was always the six of us. We would often just go to the movies, because it was not that much to do in those days.

One day, we rode by a house in a nice community where mostly school teachers lived. Herb and I pointed out one particular house that we liked (thinking that was the same type of house we were going to have one day).

All six of us spent a lot of time together, mostly because only one of the guys had a car. We even went to Senior Prom together.

I remember there being a teacher that liked me in school. He was just out of college and I ignored him only because I could not believe a teacher would like me. He gave me his number and I talked with him a few times; but, I stayed away from him. I didn't realize he really cared for me until Senior Prom, when he walked over to me saying he heard I was engaged, looking at my finger to see the ring. If I hadn't had such low self esteem, I could have waited until I graduated to date him. I did not have a class with him; but, when I would see him in the hall he would always look so disappointed.

In the fifties, I had limited dreams and thoughts about what I wanted to do or be as an adult. How could I? Most of my life was spent being a mother to my niece and my brother.

One of my girlfriends wanted to go to California and be in the movies; but, at 18, right out of school, I found out I was pregnant. I immediately told Herb who said, "Ok, we have to get married."

Now, I didn't really know what it meant to be married, as there was no one I could talk to. In my community or household, you just didn't talk about certain things. The only thing I could think about was that it was a grand opportunity to get away from home; so, Herb and I set the date for the first week in July.

My mother went and talked with the pastor of the church, Reverend M.L. Raglin. For whatever reason Herb said he had to change the date to the middle of July. My mother found out and said to me, "That nigga ain't going to marry you, and I am not going to embarrass myself by going back to the church."

So, I went to make an appointment with the pastor. I didn't tell my mother the date, but I told my dad. The day we were to be married my mother was standing on the steps of the church, and because I hadn't told her, I didn't know what to think. I just got out of the taxi and waited for my dad. Only my mother and my dad were there to see Herb and I get married.

Right after we got married and left the church, we went over to my dad's and celebrated with him and his lady friend. They lived in that same one room place that he was in when I ran away from home as a teenager.

I just kept thinking to myself, "Wow, I was finally free from my mother." I thought that because I really did get married to move away from home. This was the only way I could see to leave.

We stayed at my dad's until almost morning, then went to a hotel for two days before moving into Herb's mother's house (where only his mother and sister lived).

His sister was an adult, but she was in a wheelchair. She was a very nice and sweet lady. She did most of the cooking and cleaning – all while in her wheelchair.

After I married, my two friends and I never got together again. Herb's two friends met other girls. We eventually became friends with Naomi (a girl I knew in high school) and her husband. They lived within walking distance of us.

Our first year of marriage was good. Herb and I spent a lot of time together. There was not much to do, so we would go to the movies twice a week. We had our first child – a baby girl (while still living with his mother). That brought us lots of joy.

His mother and sister took good care of me after I had the baby; but, then we moved into our own apartment. This is when I began to see what a windstorm actually looked and felt like.

Being out of Herb's mother's house, I guess he felt he had freedom to expose his temper. I could not believe his behavior most times, and really couldn't believe that I would be experiencing in my marriage the same things I ran away from home for. I was very afraid of my husband (the same as I was of my mother). What had I gotten myself into?

He had a deep baritone voice that could be frightening in itself. He would often come home from work angry and fussing, and then reclean the house (polishing furniture again), even after I already cleaned up. He would even check the baby to see if I bathed her clean enough. One day he came home and looked at the baby and she was wet; so, he yelled at me and swung at me. I ran in the bathroom and locked the door. He left the house and went around the corner to our friends' house.

I was too timid to say anything. I had no experience in violence. I never knew how to fight. A huff and a puff and my fantasy home had come down.

He talked about having a baby boy. I actually thought if I had a boy, that would make him happy. And, seeing how I wasn't on any birth control at the time, I actually became pregnant (at the age of 20) with our second child.

I remember our lights getting turned off at Christmas time (while I was pregnant). We ended up having to spend Christmas day at a friend's house, because Herb took the money to buy a new jacket for himself, instead of paying the light bill. His first priority seemed to always be himself. He liked to party and dress well.

A few weeks later, two men from Kay Jewelers came to the house to repossess my wedding ring for non-payment. I just gave the rings to them. I didn't know Herb was not paying the bill. Next, the rental office served a warrant on us to move out in three days. I immediately went to his part-time job asking him what we were going to do. He said he didn't have any money and kept working.

I went back home and called the furniture store to come pick up the furniture, because he hadn't paid the bill on that either. And, also, because there was nowhere to store the furniture, and because I did not want the embarrassment of my furniture sitting out on the street.

Feeling left out of options at about six or seven months into this pregnancy, I found myself going to Herb's mother's house, who said I could stay as long as I needed to. I thanked her; but, said I think it would be best if I started planning to go home to my own mother.

Herb went to the club as I sat on his mother's front porch all night long wondering where my life was going. I found myself not wanting to live any longer; but, I thought about my child and my unborn baby. I even thought about how badly I reeaaalllllyyy did NOT want to go back home, seeing how I had promised myself I would never go back to my mother's house. But, I guess, you can't always say never because you never know what might happen (and by this time I was now eight months pregnant).

Humbled in spirit, I called my mother asking if I could come back home, and she quickly said, yes. I think she actually liked the fact that I was having to come back home, because her statement to me was, "I knew it!"

My marriage with Herb got real interesting after that. He'd bring me money, and then come back in two days and ask for it back. And, yes, I'd give the money back to him. You may be asking, why? Well, I did not want him causing a problem at my mother's house. You see, he had become really arrogant and loud. I remember one night we were sitting on the bed talking at my mother's house when all of a sudden, he threatened that he would take our daughter and our unborn baby because I was unfit to be a mother. I started crying and remember jumping on him until the bed slat fell. I think I lost it, because I believed him.

My mother told him to leave and she said to me that night and, I quote, "You are crazy to believe a nigger wants to raise any children. Give them to him and see. Stop crying and do what you need to do. Go to the courthouse and take out a warrant for nonsupport." And, grudgingly, that's exactly what I did.

After the baby was born and we found out it was a boy, I named him, Herbert; but, we called him Ricky.

Unfortunately, because I kept seeing and having relations with Herb, I found out I was pregnant again. Now, I'm twenty-one or two, and I said to my husband, "until you bring me a key to an apartment that you have rented, we have nothing else to say to each other." I think I was sick and tired of being sick and tired.

Shortly after our third child, Anthony, was about nine months old, I heard that Herb had left Atlanta. I went then and filed for a legal separation, and eventually divorced him.

Some years later, while my eldest daughter, Philanda, who we called Banana, was a senior in high school, she asked if I knew where her father lived. I didn't know, but I gave her his mother's phone number. His mother called him, and he called Banana and came to Atlanta for her high school graduation. That's when Herb got to know his three children; and, by then, I was no longer afraid of him, as I had grown up.

I was living in a housing project with my three children, trying to figure out how to support and raise them. There was a lady named, Mrs. Hilda, in the community who offered to keep the children while I worked night shift, charging only what I could afford to give. She said to me, "You don't have to pick the kids up at night. Just let them stay the night and pick them up in the morning."

I would do that, then walk my oldest daughter to school, and afterwards come back home with the boys. I'd feed them and then take a nap.

During that time, I met several different men; but, I didn't have the time nor the energy to invest in a new relationship. In my head I thought no man would want a woman with three children anyway. Later, I came to believe this after meeting a man who was introduced to me by a guy friend.

I saw him for about six months and every week, when he saw me he always gave me money. I never asked for anything – for one reason because I was not used to asking anyone for money. So, wow, he was impressive. Little did I know...that was bait.

At first, I wasn't aware he was married. I tried to break it off with him, because he became so jealous, which made me afraid of him. I could not even go out with my brother without him accusing me of going out to meet someone. I started night school with my neighbor, because I needed that one unit to receive my diploma and my neighbor needed one year to finish high school, too. I told him because of this, I wouldn't be home at night, and he then accused me of going in the front door of the school and leaving out the back door.

You see, to him, I was considered a good girl who didn't get drunk and use foul language. Because of this, I knew I had to figure out a way to get rid of him...to make him leave me alone. So, my plan was to have my brother, Lamar, who was a heavy drinker, come over to my house and drink all the beer and gin, and leave the cans and bottles on the table. Then, I would start cursing and acting like I was losing my mind. This eventually led the guy to drifting away and leaving me alone. After that I did not want to see alcohol again.

About a year later, I met another man. Some friends would come over on Saturdays and this particular Saturday, they brought a man with them by the name of Sid. He was very insistent and persistent. He would often joke pretending that we were related, because I had the same last name (Smith). I never officially gave him my phone number. He saw the number on my telephone, which is how he started calling me.

We started a relationship after months of phone conversations and friendship. He was nice and very funny. I liked that because he always made me laugh. This was something new for me. I also learned that he had been in the military, was working a few different jobs, and had a car. I had never met a man who appeared to have everything together. Well, what did I know anyway? I thought he really liked me the way I liked him.

He told me he would always respect my children, so when he would come to see me he would always leave before midnight. He was very quick thinking and I was fairly young and kind of naive, so the lines he used on me were new (to me).

I used to have a small refrigerator with an 18-inch freezer. After taking me grocery shopping one day, he found out that my freezer couldn't hold all of the food he had bought. A few weeks later, he was taking me to the store to buy a refrigerator with a larger freezer. That was moving pretty fast to me. I had never received gifts like that from a man.

I found myself moving out of the projects into an apartment complex where my father was the resident manager. Sid bought me new furniture, even though he didn't have much money. I really thought I was in love. Even after living together, he'd still always leave before the kids woke up (although I think they probably knew he was there).

One of the jobs Sid had was with Ford Motor Company, working side-by-side with my brother, Lester. Later he got a job with Delta Airlines, which is when he told me that he had put me down as his wife and the children down as his children (since my maiden name was Smith and his name was Smith). We weren't married, so we didn't know how and/or if that was even going to work.

A while later, he came down with a cold, which turned into a really bad cough. That cough lasted so long that we finally went to the doctor. Many tests were run, afterwards revealing that he had tuberculosis. He was going to have to go to a state hospital in Rome, Georgia until it cleared up (which we were told could be months or years). Neither one of us knew what that meant.

He was always afraid of doctors; so, he decided before he left for the hospital that we should get married. Just in case something happened to him, he said I'd have a marriage license for the insurance at Delta. So, we went to the courthouse and got married; then, I went home and told my children that we got married. I didn't think about how that sounded to my six, seven and eight-year old kids; but, they just said, okay.

Sid stayed in the hospital for about one year. I'd go and visit him every other week and when his step-mother and father would visit from Cleveland, Ohio, we'd all go together.

When they dismissed him as being clear of tuberculosis, we were able to then continue our so called "happy life" together. He went back to Delta where we got to fly fairly often to visit my sister, Jackie, in New Jersey and his family in Ohio. The children liked this because we flew first class. I found it funny how we only flew to see those particular family members; but, I didn't mind. He was a good provider.

He always made sure I had transportation to get to important events. He didn't attend any of the events with me, like football banquets, or games; but, he'd always buy everything we needed.

I remember going to the doctor for my routine physical and was cautioned that because I had been on birth control for a very long time, and because I smoked cigarettes, there was a double chance of me having a heart attack. I decided– at that point – to let my body rest from the birth control pills for a few months. After telling Sid this, all he said was, "Well."

I responded, "Well, what if I get pregnant?"

He simply replied, "O. K."

I actually thought I was sterile by then, because I had been on birth control pills for so long; but, I quickly found out I wasn't. I became pregnant with my fourth child, Shundra, within only four or five months.

Around that same time, I started seeing signs that Sid was seeing other women. I'd find receipts in his pockets for charges of women's items, hotels, and restaurants. He even came home one day saying, "Let's go out to dinner. I need to talk to you." I was about five or six months pregnant at that time.

He started the conversation off by telling me that two detectives had come to his job at Delta asking him if he was married. He said he told them he was, which afterwards, they asked if his wife knew he was married. And, before he got to say, no, they advised him to tell his wife because they were serving him with child support papers.

I was hurt, surprised, and confused. He told me he had not been married before when I asked him earlier in our relationship. Now, he says – in his mind –he had not been married. I pointed out that legally he had been and began to question everything about him.

Who was he? I called his aunt in Ohio and said, "I'm married and having a baby and I don't even know this man. What is his real name, and does he have a wife?" She said you might want to talk to his father.

Sid's father and step-mother came to visit after our baby was born. His step-mother told me that she and his father had discussions about me and had decided that I needed to know some things. I learned he had been married and had twin sons, but one had died. And, because the ex-wife could not find him, she had mailed the divorce papers to his father's house. My husband never knew about it though.

The child was living in New Jersey, and I don't believe I had ever met him. As a matter of fact, I don't believe Sid ever contacted him, nor did he want to talk about him; but, I – nonetheless – always made sure his child support payments were made.

I also learned later from his cousin that he had a daughter by another woman whom he didn't marry. This daughter was older than the twin son I found about earlier, and lived in Cleveland, Ohio. I never knew that child either.

When Shundra, our daughter, was about four or five years old, he told me he had another son that we were going to pick up from the airport. I said to myself, I probably need to have a talk with him at that very moment, as that, too, was a surprise to me. And, on top of that, the son was in his late twenties and was coming to live with us, along with his wife and child.

They lived with us for about six months until they got their own apartment; but, later they moved back to Cleveland. Even though Sid's son came to Georgia, they never really developed a relationship.

Shortly after that, another surprise surfaced. I found out from Sid's father that his middle name wasn't his middle name. This meant his middle name on Shundra's birth certificate wasn't his middle name. The more I visited Cleveland and talked with different family members the more secrets were revealed. As for my thoughts, I'm not sure why I continued to stay with him; but, I never really had a lot of trust. Some of the things his step mother told me, I kept to myself, because she asked me to. She also noted that I should keep my eyes open at all times, because things may not be exactly what they appear to be.

He was always the life of the party, a free spirit, and a braggart in several ways. He'd give you the impression that he had more money than he actually did (mostly because he was spending bill money). He would even drink more than everyone in the room, but would never seem to get drunk. Then, came the women. He had a very strong weakness for women. Some he'd bring to the house saying they were just co-workers. Some I didn't have a good feeling about and told him they couldn't come back.

I left him three times during our 17 years of marriage; but found myself going back to him each time. One of those times, I actually divorced him; but, then remarried him later. Don't ask me why. He was quite skilled in mind control and manipulation. He even said to me once (when Shundra was in her baby bed), "You know, I could through this baby out of this window!"

I jumped up crying, "Please don't hurt my baby. If you don't want us, just leave!! Please leave us!!"

He would say all kinds of crazy things. I would pray and beg God to please let him leave and never come back, because it never occurred to me that I could leave. I guess that is what happens when you are not in control of your own mind (I'm sure I'm not the only one that's been there or is there now).

Another instance of crazy things was during one of our separate periods (December 1976). It was a freezing and spine-chilling night. I remember him calling me saying he wanted to talk to me. I was cooking, so I told the kids I was going out to the car to talk to him. I put on a long leather and fur coat with a full fur lining to make sure I was prepared for the weather's chill.

When I got into the car and closed the door, he immediately speeds out of the complex, which led me to shouting, "Where are you going?! Let me out!" His only words to me were, "If I can't have you, no one else will."

After that, he had made a left turn, and I was either thrown or pushed out of the car onto the curve. I saw the car drive straight into a ditch. As I laid on the ground, I found myself drifting in and out of consciousness. I just knew I was dying.

When my eyes would be forced to close, I would drift into blackness. It was so black. I kept fighting to keep my eyes open and prayed to God, "Lord, I cannot die. My children won't have anybody to raise them." And, when I opened my eyes again, there was a man standing over me. I also heard Sid's voice (from afar) saying, "My wife, my wife." I remember whispering to the guy standing over me, "please don't let him come near me."

The paramedics showed up shortly after that and I remember being taken to the hospital, which is when I actually saw Sid again. He was standing in a distance, but didn't come closer because a policewoman was questioning me, asking if Sid had pushed me out of the car. I told her I couldn't remember if he pushed me or not.

I survived that accident with a few scratches and bruises (although I did have to wear a neck brace for a while). Every day after the accident, however, I found myself drinking more than I usually would. I've always casually and socially drank; but, the level of drinking I was doing at this time was something much more. I thought I needed a drink to hold on to life and I thought that was my only resort.

At first, I was drinking because I liked the taste of beer and champagne; but, I also drank to get high and to numb the pain of life (not knowing what to do or how to do it). I was moving along in life; but, the only goal I had was to live long enough to see each of my children graduate from high school. In my mind, if they graduated from high school, they could live on their own and take care of themselves. I only felt the need to live long enough to get them ready for adult life.

Later, I began having stomach pains, so I went to the doctor, where I was diagnosed with gallstones. I had to have surgery within 30 days, which had me worried. I didn't feel that was enough time to prepare, and I didn't have any insurance coverage. Plus, I wouldn't be able to provide for the children if I couldn't work.

Coincidently, Sid called me.

He asked me how I was doing, and somehow, I found myself having the conversation about us getting back together again. I told him I didn't want to talk about that because I had stuff on my mind. He wanted to know *what* was on my mind, and I told him about the surgery. He told me that I was still covered under his Delta insurance, and that I should come and move back in. He said I had nothing to worry about, in his normal, fast-talking way. He covered all of this before I could even breathe or say one word.

My oldest daughter (who was home from the Air Force) heard the conversation and said to me, "Why not? Just do it." I didn't want to go back to him; but, I thought I didn't have a choice. What a wrong and dreadful decision.

He hired a truck and some men to pack up my furniture and move me back into his house. I went back to him and we became a couple once again. This time I really didn't like him anymore. Thirty days later, I went into the hospital for double surgery. I had to have my gallbladder removed first, and then my gynecologist removed some tumors, which ended up being a seven-hour surgery. After the surgery I healed well with no complications.

One of my close girlfriends who used to be my drinking partner told me she went to a church and got saved. That meant I no longer had a drinking companion, which led me to asking her for the name of her church.

About six weeks after my surgery I went to her church (which was actually right up the street from where I lived) to attend Bible Study. It was at this Bible Study that I heard the Word of God for the first time. This was so enlightening to me, because I would have thought I would have heard His voice sooner (seeing how I was raised in the church). The teacher was teaching about Salvation:

I am the door: by me if any man enters in, he shall be saved, and shall go in and out, and find pasture. The thief cometh not, but for to steal, and to kill, and to destroy: I am come that they might have life, and that they might have it more abundantly. John 10: 9 -10 KJV

I was led a few weeks later to receive Christ as my personal Savior, and noticed my whole life beginning to change.

When I started applying everything that I was learning in Bible Study, my husband began disliking me more and more. He said he liked "the old me...the drinking me...the me who would curse him out." But, I was learning to control those things and was growing out of that behavior.

The women who would constantly call the house couldn't make me leave anymore (I used to pack up and leave when they would call). He couldn't provoke me to anger anymore, which upset him so much that he ended up leaving me; but, not before calling me crazy and telling my mother that I was now strange. Funny how I was not a bit surprised to learn that she actually agreed with him. It didn't matter, though.

That was the final time we divorced and the last time we would be together.

Walking in Faith

But they that wait upon the Lord shall renew their strength; they shall mount up with wings as eagles; they shall run, and not be weary; and they walk and not faint.
Isaiah 40:31 NIV

I had an excellent work ethic; but, no skills. I mostly did warehouse work. After my oldest daughter joined the Air Force and my next son, Ricky, joined the Army, my house was emptying fast. Anthony was starting to make a life for himself, leaving only my youngest child at home.

I worked at a chemical company. I didn't have any skills, so my position choices were either in the warehouse or as a dishwasher. I chose warehouse and was packing boxes of soap. I then moved from that to silk screening labels. For the first time, I could say I had acquired a skill and a title. I was a Silk Screen Operator.

A while later the employees at the chemical company went on strike, which I walked in for a while, as well.

Unfortunately, because the strike lasted too long, I was led to start seeking other employment.

I was hired at another chemical company that originally wanted me as a supervisor of their screening department; I declined that position because I didn't want to manage people.

My references were very high, so the company knew I could handle the job. I was an excellent worker, but was afraid and uncomfortable with accepting a leadership position. My esteem was low; and despite all of this, the company still wanted me. They called me the next week and asked me if I would take the position and not be a supervisor? I said, yes. I needed a job.

After two weeks of working there, I realized that the screening department was a mess. It was unorganized, ink was everywhere, and the silk screens were half washed and had to be cleaned before using again. Something had to change. The manager asked me again about taking the supervisor position, and I was – then – pleased to accept it. The workers received me fairly well.

After a few years, I was moved to the packaging area because of remodeling on the screening side of the building. This was very challenging because as gallon-sized jugs were filled and sent down the conveyor belt, I'd have to put them in the box. Then, another worker would fill those jugs so fast that I found myself not being able to keep up. I would ask her to slow down, and every time she would say, no, and continue working at her same pace. I thought she was so mean.

One day I walked away to take a break and passed by the print shop and found myself staring into the window. I was fascinated with the printing press, and asked the lady who ran that press if it was hard. She told me it was really hard. So, I went back to work, again struggling to keep up with the flow.

As I'm working, the question: "Is this what you want to be doing for the rest of your life?" came to me so strongly that I almost answered out loud. I couldn't get that print press off my mind; so, the next week I went to Atlanta Area Technical School to inquire about their printing classes. They didn't call the class "Printing", but instead Graphic Arts.

I registered to attend night classes and started learning printing as well as graphics. I didn't tell anyone I was in school for about three weeks, until my manager called me into his office asking if I would like to try out for the print shop. I immediately said, yes, informing him that I was in school at night. "Oh?" He asked, "what are you studying?" I said, "Offset Printing."

There were two machines in the print shop and one person already there who ran the two-color press. The manager told that person to supervise and train me; but, she didn't know I was in school for graphic arts and offset printing. She would tell me the wrong things to do and then she would criticize all my work. I went through some extremely tough times working with her; but, something happened between she and the manager and they moved her to another area. I was sent to outside training for proper use of the two-color press, which I mastered. They later moved a lady by the name of Mrs. Hazel Irvin from the warehouse to the print shop to help out.

I knew her because we worked together in the warehouse years before; but, when we were placed together in that shop, we became very close. She was trained to enter the work orders into the computer for me to print. We had an excellent working relationship, and both were learning something new. I was so inspired and learned so much from her wisdom. We had a lot of time to ourselves to talk about whatever we chose behind closed doors.

I remember I was once thinking about looking for another job, and while still dealing with fear and insecurities, Mrs. Hazel told me, "Try anyway. They are either going to say yes or no." So, I applied for a job at MARTA, and she prayed for me and with me. Afterwards, I found out I had the job. Mrs. Hazel was like a mother, a mentor, a wise counselor and a friend through many of my life's events and challenges, rejoicing at all of my triumphs.

I left the chemical company and entered into a whole new challenge with eight years of pressure and harassment. The new job was determined that make new hires conform to the workers in that print shop; but, I came in well-qualified, so that was not going to happen to me. My skills and work ethics prevailed.

I started college in 1994. My intention was to take a class that would help me teach Sunday School better; but, after I registered they sent me to the Dean's Office to see Dr. James B. Keiller. He asked me if I had taken any college courses before. I said, no. He then suggested the first two classes required for a Degree. Now this may sound crazy; but, I was scared and unaware that I was entering a four-year college.

Dr. James B. Keiller had such a calming demeanor that it made me calm. After I left his office I figured I would still just take a few classes. Mrs. Hazel was right there with me. When I went to the first banquet at Beulah Heights Bible College she was there, as well.

Entering college was extremely challenging for me because of my limited foundation and my missing so many days of school as a teenager. Not to mention, my transcript that had D's and maybe two C's. At that time all four of my children were on their own, which freed me from worrying about those responsibilities; but, even with what I believed God was leading me into, I continued to be scared. I pressed on anyway – struggling, but still pressing.

You're probably asking why was I so challenged? Because, I didn't know how to do what was required and really didn't know where to turn to get the help I needed. I knew how to pray, however, and that's exactly what I did.

> *And it shall come to pass, that before they call, I will answer; and while they are yet speaking, I will hear. (Isaiah 65:24)*

My manager saw me in the lunch room one day studying and asked what I was doing. I was reluctant to share that I was in school because I didn't want to face any more persecution. Being my manager, however, he was aware of the problems in that work place; so, I told him I was in school. He persisted in knowing what I was doing and how I was doing, so I ended up letting him know that I was struggling. Surprisingly, he offered to help and volunteered to meet with me twice a week at McDonald's to tutor me. Later, God gave me favor with the secretary to the general manager and she offered to type my papers. I printed the letterhead and business cards for the company; so, she would bring me her order in a folder and I would hand her my work in a folder and no one ever knew what was happening. She wouldn't charge me a dime. All she asked was that I pray for her and be her friend. We did this for two years until I had another interruption of shock and embarrassment in my life.

There I was teaching Sunday School and volunteering at shelters, and from out of nowhere, my son was being accused of child abuse. I saw his picture plastered all over the front page of the daily newspaper and all over the TV stations. This saddened me because I knew – firsthand – how the media can blow things up before they get the full truth.

Cameras were following me in and out of the courthouse. My two daughters would hide my face with umbrellas. I would go to work, to church and around the community only to experience whispers and looks of mockery. It was painful hearing what my son was facing. My daughters and I were praying that God would intervene.

We found out my son's wife turned on him because her former boyfriend told her to. He wasn't trying to hurt her; but he wanted to put my son away for life. His plot was to have his son lie and accuse my son of abuse. My son lost five years out of his life due to these false accusations.

I felt so overwhelmed I almost quit school; but, there was a will inside of me that pushed on. The pressure was so great at work, I thought that I'd quit the job before I quit school. The supervisor would make me work late, which made me late for school at times. It had gotten to a point where I had to choose between work and school. So, because I couldn't be late for class, I choose school.

I resigned my position, gave up my apartment, put my furniture in storage and then asked God, "what next?" The answer was to go introduce myself to the vice president of the school, Dr. Benson M. Karanja. I introduced myself as a student, and apologized for meeting him under such circumstances. I told him I had three days to find a place to live. Later I filed bankruptcy. He sent me to his secretary to prepare me for a dormitory room. This was totally new to me. I had never lived in one room and shared a bathroom. I was in my late fifties and somehow, I was at peace. All I needed were my books and my computer.

My mother was convincing my family and my adult children that I was now crazy. They backed off and had nothing to do with me. I tried to understand how my children (who were raised with me and knew me) could actually listen to someone plant seeds of evil in their minds (just to pull them closer to her). It all came down to money. Money that I could not give. That hurt deeply sometimes, because I felt all I had were my children.

Nonetheless, I had to move on...even though I found myself struggling to make it in school. It was really hard. I even started to think that maybe I *was* losing my mind; but, I honestly believed I was moving by faith.

Two of my children had yet to decide to be a part of my life, but I remained hopeful that one day they will come back. Until then, I had to keep pressing down the path God was leading me.

I later received a Certificate in Bible, Associates of Arts Degree in 1999 in Biblical Studies and a Bachelor of Arts degree in 2002 in Biblical Education. That same year I was ordained Elder and Associate Minister of Cosmopolitan AME Church in Atlanta.

On December 24, 2013, I received a phone call and heard a voice asking, "May I speak to Ann?"

I said, "This is she."

"Merry Christmas. This is Lonnie."

I happily replied, "Lonnie Warren?!" He said, yes. It was as if time had stood still. "How did you find me?!" I asked, excitedly.

He said he had been looking for me for years and could not find anyone who knew my whereabouts? So, he had his oldest son try to find me on the internet? He called several numbers and finally got the right one. It was as if I had just seen him a week ago; but, it had been at least 40 years. We dated when we were younger, and now, we were both 70.

We met up on Christmas Day and went to The Varsity where we sat, ate and talked for four hours. We saw each other almost every day after that and talked every night. I was getting over a broken wrist and had been taking care of Mother for the past two years, before she passed away.

About a month later, Lonnie and I were sitting in my living room watching TV and Lonnie would do what he always did...talk and keep me laughing. Then, he said, "You may not love me now, but you will later."

I asked him, "What do you mean?"

He replied, "I lost you once; but, I won't let that happen again. We'll be married."

I asked him, "What are you saying? Are you asking me to marry you?"

He said, "Yes! Do I need to get on one knee? But, you don't have to answer right now."

I sensed at that moment that he felt like he had just asked the wrong question, so I said, "When a person asks you a question like that it deserves an answer NOW...and my answer is, YES!"

A week later we started looking at rings and began planning our life together. The night we picked the rings up, he placed it on my finger. And, since neither of us drank alcohol, I got two champagne glasses and filled them with ginger ale and we made a toast to each other and to our future. Then, we hugged each other and cried.

He informed me that he needed to have surgery on his shoulder, which is why he couldn't hold me as tight as he wanted to. I told him, "If you hold me any tighter, I won't be able to breathe."

It was amazing how quickly he and his doctors worked to coordinate his entire surgery process. He always said to me, "One day soon I'm going to give you a good squeeze."

We continued to talk on the phone until midnight the night before surgery. After seeing what time it was, I told him we should hang up because his surgery was at seven in the morning. He made me promise I would come over to his house after he came home from surgery.

About 8:30 am that morning, his niece, Sheila, called me asking if I was alone. I replied, yes; but, somehow knew she was calling with bad news. She informed me that Lonnie had a heart attack while on his way to the hospital (to have his surgery performed), and he didn't survive. I was devastated. The grief – at times – was unbearable...so much so that I didn't think I would survive. All I could say was, "BUT, GOD."

I began to question God during this time. How could He allow this to happen to 'true love'? I had to realize, however, that God allowed Lonnie and I to experience real love for the first time in our lives. He allowed us to talk about living a life of forever together. We just knew we had more time.

After only a short reunion, on April 24, 2014, I lost the love of my life. He was such a special man, and of course, it was a tremendous blow. I must admit, however, that experiencing real, genuine love and spending as much time as we did together was priceless. It was as if we were compelled to enjoy every moment we could together. I missed him greatly.

The next year for my birthday, Shundra said, "Mommy, since so many of your dreams haven't come true, I want to fulfill your childhood dream of going to Paris."

I was a bit surprised, but immediately went and applied for my passport. We flew first class with Shundra and her friend, Krisie. The plane was huge. We had our own individual bed to lie in and when Shundra told the flight attendant it was my birthday, upon exiting the plane, they gave us a bottle of champagne as a gift.

As a little girl, I always envisioned Paris to be a place of love. Paris was all that I had dreamed. The atmosphere was calming, peaceful, and people were walking around holding hands. Shundra and I held hands, as well. She didn't want us to get separated being amongst the many people in Paris who were walking fast and focused.

I enjoyed shopping in Paris, too. The prices were actually reasonable. I remember having to cut our tourism short on some days, though, because my knee was giving me a lot of pain (due to how cold it was there). But, oh, how I was determined to keep pressing on other days. And why wouldn't I? I was in Paris!!

The night lights were a breathtaking sight to remember; and the "Sweet Shop" across the street from the hotel was absolutely delicious. We visited there so much that the servers recognized me when I walked in, greeting me with a "hello, mom; I have your order ready."

During our last two days of being in France, we traveled to London. I remember almost falling when trying to get out of the taxi at the Queens castle, cause my knee was hurting badly; it was so cold.

When entering the hotel in London, we were surprised to see a party going on in the lounge. We heard the band playing and people singing Stevie Wonder's version of "Happy Birthday," and thought it was funny because we initially thought they were singing to me (since it was my birthday).

Realizing that the party was for someone else, Shundra informed the desk clerk that it was my birthday, too. This prompted all of the clerks behind the desk to beautifully sing, "Happy Birthday" to me. I felt so special. Paris and London were both experiences I will remember forever.

My Inspiration

I am only but a man, human in nature...
Not a God, not a king.
But, if I was to become a king,
You would surely be my queen.

I have feelings and needs. I love, I hate.
The feelings of love need to come up to date.
It's easy to hate. It's hard to love.
One must understand...what is love?

When two people – one male,
One female, together share...
Feelings of joy, emotions, times of happiest,
Relating to one another on the best of topics.

To share intimate feelings with each other...
Feeling of making one another happy.

Seeing the sparkle in one's eyes
when you look into them...
Feeling the pounding in your chest
when you're with your lover,

*Saying that 'I love you' and meaning it...
having it returned.*

*The words you hear are from my heart.
You won't hear them on the radio,
or read them on any card.
These thoughts come from my heart.*

Ric

****

Herbert LaCoste Clemons (Ricky), my second-born, entered into this world on November 7, 1961. He was a quiet and timid child who loved watching cartoons and playing with his favorite toy Army men. He wasn't very active as a child; but, he was very smart.

He taught himself how to write and draw. Drawing, I believe, brought him peace. Whenever he would get angry about something, he'd always go find paper and a pencil and start drawing. His favorite to draw were black super heroes that he created from his own imagination.

In addition to teaching himself how to draw, Ricky also taught himself Karate, and even made his own Karate chucks. While attending Fredrick Douglas High School, he took interest in the ROTC and became a part of the Drill Team. He liked it so much that he later joined the United States Army.

Although not a great communicator, Ricky was a brilliant thinker. He was patient with people and enjoyed working in the community. He would drive senior citizens and the disabled around when they had errands to run. During many of those errands, I remember him dropping by my house, getting some water or soda out of the refrigerator, walking in every room, and then saying, "See you later, Mom. I was only saying hi and bye". I enjoyed his presence.

On January 8, 2013, while at Shundra's house, Anthony, called. He informed us that he was headed to Ricky's house. Ricky's girlfriend had called saying Ricky had flatlined. I had no idea what that meant.

Shundra asked me, "Do you know where he lives?"

I said, "Yes."

"Well, let's go!!"

When we arrived at Ricky's apartment, we saw police, detectives, my great nephew, Ricky's girlfriend and others.

As I got out of the car, one of the detectives approached me saying, "You must be the mother?"

When I said yes, he asked for ID and told me that they were waiting for the coroner. I asked what happened and the detective told me Ricky was deceased, and when someone dies at home they must wait for the coroner. I could tell the detective was being very sympathetic as he continued to explain how when a death occurs at home, an autopsy has to be done to determine the cause of death. He also told me to not worry if we didn't have life insurance for my son, because the State will bury him for free. The detective concluded by asking that I call him in two days.

I lost it right then.

Shortly after, I saw Anthony and Shundra walking over to me. Shundra said, "Mommy, get in the car. They are bringing him out." (Shundra is very protective of me). As I sat in the car, God spoke to me saying, "You brought him into the world and now you watch him leave." I then stepped out of the car and watched them bring my son down those steps in a white body bag, and put him into a white van.

While I was preparing and making arrangements for Ricky's funeral, I found out that I also had family members trying to do the same thing – behind my back. But, seeing how I was the mother, they could not take control. This whole experience was very traumatic for me, as it happened so sudden. Everything that I had to deal with was painful and through it all, I'm grateful that Shundra never left me. I'm also thankful to God for giving me the strength to see that my son's obituary and funeral arrangements were handled decently and in order. That was therapy for me.

A few weeks after Ricky's funeral, I found a stack of old letters written by Ricky that I had saved all of these years. I started reading the letters and remembering how he would talk to me, and asking me questions about how my life was as a black woman in the 60's, left to raise children with so little to work with. As I continued reading his words, the words that he wrote to me (his mother) comforted me greatly. He said, "I can only write from my heart." Of course, as with any child, Ricky was not a son without faults; but, his heart was golden.

One of the most cherished attributes I hold dear about Ricky is his undying and unwavering love for me, his mother. No matter what I was going through, he always encouraged me; and though I've already mentioned him plenty of times as being the inspiration behind this book, I want the world to know how talented, blessed and wonderful my son, Herbert LaCoste Clemons, really was.

I've included a letter he wrote to me on Mother's Day in 1996. It touched my heart then, and still touches my heart today...

****

Dear Mom...

Hello. I'm writing you on this Mother's Day. I hope you're in the best of health and in high spirits.

I was going to buy a Mother's Day card from the store, but they ran out before I got there. But, what can Hallmark say about my mother on Mother's Day that I can't say best from my heart?

HALLMARK WAS NOT THERE when you had (9) months of pain to bring me into this world - your first son of four children.

HALLMARK WAS NOT THERE when you nursed me, and took care of me as a baby who couldn't take care of himself; but, you did it no matter how tired you were.

HALLMARK WAS NOT THERE when you entertained me when I was bored, fed me when I was hungry, or when you took time out to help me with my homework, so I was literate to knowing my opportunities and able to accomplish anything I wanted to, as an adult.

HALLMARK WAS NOT THERE when you - so many times - had to sacrifice what you wanted for your children's wants, when you kept a home environment that was best to raise us up.

HALLMARK WAS NOT THERE when you stayed by my side when I was in the United States or Germany, no matter what part of the world I was in, when I was in trouble or any times of need.

HALLMARK WAS NOT THERE when you told me to trust in the God and do the right thing, and the difference between right and wrong.

*HALLMARK WAS NOT THERE when I was born (11-7-1961).

*HALLMARK WAS NOT THERE when I went to my (first prom).

*HALLMARK WAS NOT THERE when I (graduated 9/1/1979 on time)

*HALLMARK WAS NOT THERE when I came (back from the Army 3/11/1982).

*HALLMARK WAS NOT THERE when I came (to get Married 9/26/1991).

*HALLMARK WAS NOT THERE when I got (in trouble 6/10/1993).

HALLMARK WAS NOT THERE, but you have always been there from the beginning to the end. We as black men today need to look back and take a long look at how our mothers, Queens of the Earth, took so much time to nurture us to be the Kings we are not living up to be.

"THANK YOU, MOM, FOR ALWAYS BEING THERE FOR ME."

Well, I hope this will let you know where my thoughts are on this Mother's Day. I don't get to talk with or see you as much as I would like to, but when you get the time, I would like to see you. Happy Mother's Day.

Love, Ric

Photos

Me at 6 Years Old...

Me in 9th Grade...

VIRGINIA A. SMITH

Me in 11th Grade...

Me as 12th Grade Queen...

VIRGINIA A. SMITH

My Mother, Fannie Lou Smith...

My Father, Walter Allen Smith...

My Son, Herbert LaCoste Clemons...

Me and the Love of My Life, Lonnie Warren...

My Calling

*The Spirit of the Sovereign Lord is on me, because
the Lord has anointed me to proclaim good news
to the poor. He has sent me to bind up the brokenhearted,
to proclaim freedom for the captives and
release from darkness for the prisoners...*
Isaiah 61:1 NIV

Throughout this book, you have read repeatedly about my passion for Sunday School. I have always attended Sunday School. In my late thirties, I remember the superintendent and Sunday School teacher of my church asking me one Sunday morning if I was ready to start teaching Sunday School.

I originally said, no, and remember being aggravated that she had even asked that question. I also found it interesting how I was unable to let her question and the answer I replied with go. I found myself wrestling day in and day out about whether or not I should teach Sunday School – so much so that I was one day led by the Holy Spirit to go ahead and say, "yes."

I went back to my Sunday School teacher and told her I would take over the class...and felt instant relief. It was like a huge weight had been lifted off my chest and I was finally at peace. This let me know that my decision was in line with God's plan, and that made me feel good.

After teaching Sunday School for several years, I was promoted to Sunday School Coordinator where I was also led to begin visiting local women's shelters. I found myself teaching and praying with many of the ladies in these shelters, and later began working with missionaries, training them in Bible studies.

During those times, I remember several evangelists coming up to me stating I needed to attend biblical training classes with them. I used to always wonder why they were approaching me, until one particular evangelist said to me, "I see a calling on your life; but, I'm not one to press." Interestingly, other ministers and elders noted the same thing to me, some even asking, "why are you running from your calling?"

While studying homework one day, I noticed that I kept feeling a drawing to pick up my bible and read it. I remember pouring oil on the top of my head and began reading the book of Isaiah (Chapter 61:1 NIV). After reading this verse and remainder of the chapter, I immediately fell to the floor and began praying, realizing that I had just received my calling. Well, I somewhat knew before then; but, I did not acknowledge it until now.

I remember being scared; but, as soon as I told my pastor, the late Reverend Oliver Saxby, of my calling, he allowed me to preach a trial sermon. Afterwards, I was admitted into the Conference where I then started the process of ministering in the "African Methodist Episcopal Church".

My daughter, Shundra, her husband and their son attended my ordination service. It was quite humbling to know that God chose me. My experiences since then have been both rewarding and fulfilling.

I've served in such capacities as Pulpit Associate, Bible Teacher, and Congregational Care; and, spent a lot of time serving in senior centers, convalescent homes, women shelters, performing weddings, and officiating funerals, just to name a few. I shall not lie and say that these ventures were not challenging, because they were; but, I grew tremendously in my faith, my walk, and in my love for God and His people.

One of the biggest rewards I've received from being in ministry was seeing people's lives change for the better. It brought me joy to know that God was using me to make such a powerful impact through my teachings, prayers and time. I've witnessed so many persons mature and flourish into uncharted territories, with some becoming teachers themselves.

Ministry hasn't proven to be all that easy however. I've had to face many challenges, as well – being divorced, single and female.

Many of the pastors and elders didn't respect my calling, my gifts nor my non-traditional and unique ideas. They were not very encouraging and despite asking for help, many purposely gave little to no direction into helping me succeed.

But, that's ok.

Despite their efforts to see me fail, God showed me how to do everything I needed to do anyway – on time and in an orderly manner. And, this is because I serve a God whose will for my life will not fail. I am called, destined and living with a purpose...whether inside a church building or in any community, home or heart I'm led to minister to.

The Perfect Frame

*I will go before you and will level the mountains;
I will break down gates of bronze and cut through bars of
iron. I will give you hidden treasures, riches stored in
secret places, so that you may know that I am the Lord,
the God of Israel, who summons you by name.
Isaiah 45:2-3*

In Retrospect

Some say that hindsight is 20-20; but, I tend to think differently. I've come to realize that everything that I was forced to endure in my past was allowed by God. And, because of this realization, there is not one part that I would want to change.

Looking back over my life I can see clearly how every phase prepared me for where and who I am today. Every phase is likened to the stroke of a brush that painted the portrait of me. It captures every stroke of the brush that the Author of me (God) has dipped in different colors.

Early on, I could see myself developing and growing into someone I didn't know; but, someone I wanted to be. These accomplishments made me feel proud and oftentimes left me in awe, because I used to think they were impossible feats that were far beyond my reach.

I was delivered from my fear of learning, upon realizing that I could learn academically, think academically, and understand academically. This enhanced my self-image, giving me courage and a joy that I had never known, and making me stronger and stronger every day in myself.

My growth and walk in faith have enabled me to openly share my testimonies, to confidently minister unto others, to remain strong and steadfast in my thoughts, actions and ways, and to evolve into being the woman I am today...

My Father's creation...wonderfully and beautifully made.

About the Author

Virginia A. Smith is a native of Atlanta, Georgia. She is the fourth child of her parents, the late Fannie L. Smith-Vaughn and the late Walter Allen Smith. She is also the proud mother of four (two sons and two daughters), and a loving grandmother and great-grandmother.  She received her early education in the Atlanta Public School System.

Virginia's life's journey has been filled with fear, inadequacy, insecurity, timidity, low esteem and a lack of self-confidence. Having gone through many storms and disappointments, Virginia believed that surely there was more to life than what she was experiencing.

As she continued to mature and attend Sunday School, Virginia sought the Lord, and He heard her. Her Heavenly Father delivered her from all of her fears, and began transforming her life – one phase at a time. Her heart was healed, as she was learning how to grow in grace (through Christ). She began involving her time, gifts and treasures in several facets of ministry, even becoming ordained as a minister. Virginia loved teaching Sunday School and enjoyed ministering to ladies in local Women Shelters. In 2000, God gave her the words to this song, which continues to guide and drive her – even today:

> *"There's something more to **me** than I can see.*
> *There's something more to **me** than I can see.*
> *But, there's a need to be challenged*
> *that I may blossom, you see.*
> *There is something more to **me** that I can see."*

Having been strengthened through various programs, educational courses and studies, Virginia's education includes certificates in Graphic Communications, Interpersonal Communications, and Biblical Education School of the Prophets. She also earned an Associate of Arts Degree in Biblical Studies, and a Bachelors of Arts Degree in Biblical Education from Beulah Heights University. She even received a Standard Teaching Diploma from the Evangelical Training Association; and continued her studies to earn a Certificate in Small Business Management from Atlanta Technical College.

The Lord has given Virginia a heart for creating unity among women and for planting seeds in the development of His people.

THE SOLID FOUNDATION GROUP

ORDER MORE BOOKS
Mail along with payment to: **P.O. Box 1483 Smyrna, GA 30081**

Name

Address

City

State   Zip

Book		Qty	Total
	A Portrait of Virginia A. Smith by Virginia A. Smith Genre: Biography / Inspirational Cost: $13.95/each*		$
	Poetic Motifs' Significance of 9 by Kish Andes Genre: Poetry Cost: $13.95/each*		$
	How To Fade Like Griffin by Kendrick Henderson Genre: Educational Cost: $15.95/each*		$
	The Pig Who Became President By Alana Johnson Genre: Children's Cost: $12.95/each*		$
	Set Free by Truth By Amari Johnson Genre: Children's Cost: $12.95/each*		$
	Bullet Proof by Bodie Quinette Genre: Self-Help / Motivational Cost: $15.95/each*		$

 **The Cartel's Daughter Unedited: Raw and Uncut!** *by Carmine* Genre: Crime / Thriller / Urban Cost: $14.99/each*	_____	$_____

***SHIPPING & HANDLING:** *1-3 Books: $5.00* *4-9 Books: $9.00* *$3.95 each addt'l book*	_____	$_____
TOTAL ENCLOSED		$_____

Acceptable Forms of Payment: *Money orders or U.S. bank issued checks made payable to* **The Solid Foundation Group.** *Please do not send cash.*

Visit our website to learn more about our authors and their books |or| to order online.
www.TheSolidFoundationGroup.com

www.ingramcontent.com/pod-product-compliance
Lightning Source LLC
Chambersburg PA
CBHW052131010526
44113CB00034B/1678